SandCastle 2

What Do You See?

In the
Desert

Mary Elizabeth Salzmann

ABDO
Publishing Company

Published by SandCastle™, an imprint of ABDO Publishing Company, 4940 Viking Drive, Edina, Minnesota 55435.

Printed in the United States.

Cover and interior photo credits: Corel, PhotoDisc.

Library of Congress Cataloging-in-Publication Data

Salzmann, Mary Elizabeth, 1968-
    In the desert / Mary Elizabeth Salzmann.
        p. cm -- (What do you see?)
    ISBN 1-57765-564-8
        1. Deserts--Juvenile literature. [1. Deserts.] I. Title.
QH88 .S26 2001
578.754--dc21   2001022011

The SandCastle concept, content, and reading method have been reviewed and approved by a national advisory board including literacy specialists, librarians, elementary school teachers, early childhood education professionals, and parents.

Let Us Know

After reading the book, SandCastle would like you to tell us your stories about reading. What is your favorite page? Was there something hard that you needed help with? Share the ups and downs of learning to read. We want to hear from you! To get posted on the Abdo Publishing Company Web site, send us email at:

sandcastle@abdopub.com

About SandCastle™
Nonfiction books for the beginning reader

- Basic concepts of phonics are incorporated with integrated language methods of reading instruction. Most words are short, and phrases, letter sounds, and word sounds are repeated.

- Readability is determined by the number of words in each sentence, the number of characters in each word, and word lists based on curriculum frameworks.

- Full-color photography reinforces word meanings and concepts.

- "Words I Can Read" list at the end of each book teaches basic elements of grammar, helps the reader recognize the words in the text, and builds vocabulary.

- Reading levels are indicated by the number of flags on the castle.

Look for more SandCastle books in these three reading levels:

Level 1
(one flag)

Level 2
(two flags)

Level 3
(three flags)

Grades Pre-K to K
5 or fewer words per page

Grades K to 1
5 to 10 words per page

Grades 1 to 2
10 to 15 words per page

This is a desert.

It is dry and sandy.

The desert wind blows sand into piles called dunes.

The cactus is a desert plant.

This desert cactus has bright flowers.

These are Joshua trees.

Few trees grow in the desert.

Sand scorpions live in the desert.

Lizards like to sit in the hot desert sun.

This leopard lives in the desert in Asia.

What do you see in this desert?

(camels)

Words I Can Read

Nouns

A noun is a person, place, or thing

cactus (KAK-tuhss) pp. 9, 11
desert (DEZ-urt)
  pp. 5, 13, 15, 19, 21
leopard (LEP-urd) p. 19

plant (PLANT) p. 9
sand (SAND) p. 7
sun (SUHN) p. 17
wind (WIND) p. 7

Plural Nouns

A plural noun is more than one person, place, or thing

camels (KAM-uhlz) p. 21
dunes (DOONZ) p. 7
flowers (FLOU-urz) p. 11
Joshua trees
  (JOSH-oo-uh TREEZ) p. 13

lizards (LIZ-urdz) p. 17
piles (PILEZ) p. 7
scorpions
  (SKOR-pee-uhnz) p. 15
trees (TREEZ) p. 13

22

Proper Nouns

**A proper noun is the name
of a person, place, or thing**

Asia (AY-zhuh) p. 19

Verbs

A verb is an action or being word

are (AR) p. 13
blows (BLOHZ) p. 7
called (KAWLD) p. 7
do (DOO) p. 21
grow (GROH) p. 13
has (HAZ) p. 11

is (IZ) pp. 5, 9
like (LIKE) p. 17
live (LIV) p. 15
lives (LIVZ) p. 19
see (SEE) p. 21
sit (SIT) p. 17

Adjectives

An adjective describes something

bright (BRITE) p. 11
desert (DEZ-urt)
  pp. 7, 9, 11, 17
dry (DRYE) p. 5
few (FYOO) p. 13

hot (HOT) p. 17
sand (SAND) p. 15
sandy (SAND-ee) p. 5
this (THISS) pp. 11, 19, 21

23

What Do You See in the Desert?

Match the Words to the Pictures

cactus

camel

lizard

sand dunes

24